IN A PERFECT WORLD

Education

for All

Floating Schools,

Cave Classrooms,

and Backpacking

Teachers

Ron Fridell

Twenty-First Century Books
Brookfield, Connecticut

Cover photograph courtesy of Woodfin Camp & Associates (© Betty Press); Magnum Photos (© Ferdinando Scianna); Timepix (© Reuters/Claro Cortes IV).

Photographs courtesy of: Woodfin Camp & Associates: pp. 1 (© Betty Press), 16 (© Betty Press), 17 (© S. Noorani), 18 (© Betty Press), 35 (top: © Mike Yamashita), 47 (© Betty Press); © Sean Sprague/The Image Works: pp. 6, 15; AP/Wide World Photos: pp. 8, 56; Magnum Photos: pp. 25 (© Abbas), 30 (© Ferdinando Scianna), 37 (© Steve McCurry), 56 (© Chris Steele-Perkins); © Jenny Matthews/Oxfam: pp. 26, 41; © UNICEF: pp. 35 (bottom: HQ98-0448/Khoy Bona), 49 (Ethiopia/ Faye); © Charles O'Rear/Corbis: p. 36; Escuela Nueva: p. 45; Timepix: pp. 51 (© Reuters/Claro Cortes IV), 68 (© Reuters Claro Cortes IV); © Ralf-Finn Hestoft/Corbis Saba: p. 62

Maps by Mary Ellen Casey.

Library of Congress Cataloging-in-Publication Data
Fridell, Ron.
Education for all : floating schools, cave classrooms, and backpacking teachers/ Ron Fridell.
p. cm.—(In a perfect world)
Summary: Explains the lack of education in countries around the world and discusses the organizations that help children receive schooling. Includes bibliographical references and index.
ISBN 0-7613-2624-3 (lib. bdg.)
1. Basic education—Juvenile literature. 2. Education—Developing countries—Juvenile literature. [1. Education—Developing countries.]
I. Title. II. Series.
LC1035 .F75 2002
370'.9172'4—dc21
2002003305

Published by Twenty-First Century Books
A Division of The Millbrook Press, Inc.
2 Old New Milford Road
Brookfield, Connecticut 06804
http://www.millbrookpress.com

Contents

Is There Education for All?

If you were a school-age child living in a village in the Andhra Pradesh district of southern India, chances are you would not be going to school today. You would not be going to school tomorrow either, or the day after.

There is no school in this village. There are no classrooms or teachers. The nearest school is in another village 5 miles (8 km) away, and to get there, students must make their way on foot through thick forest. The school is too far away, and the journey is too dangerous. So none of the children in this village in southern India go to school. Instead they work. The girls take care of younger brothers and sisters and help their

In India and many other countries around the world, some children cannot attend school. Instead, girls work around the house while boys work outside the home to help support their families.

mothers with housework. The boys gather food in the forest and herd sheep.

There are many villages like this in India, where 30 million children do not attend school.[1] There are children just like these in villages and towns and big cities all over the world: hundreds of millions of children who never get an education, who never learn to read and write.

Most of these children will grow up illiterate. As adults, they will not be able to write their names. Instead, they may sign their names by rolling a thumb in ink and pressing it to a piece of paper. They will not be able to read a newspaper or a bus schedule. Most of them will live their lives in poverty, unable to make a decent living.

What is being done to bring education to all the children in the world who don't have it? To tell the story, we begin in New York City.

x   x   x   x

It was September 6, 2000. The new millennium had just begun. Leaders of 189 countries from all the continents of the world gathered at United Nations Headquarters in New York City for the UN Millennium Summit. They were there to look at the state of the world.

These leaders agreed that the world was far from perfect. Billions of people all over the planet were living in poverty, homeless and hungry, and dozens of nations were at war. These leaders of nations made a pledge to change all that. They declared, "We are determined to establish a just and lasting peace all over the world."[2]

But how can world peace be established?

These world leaders discussed issues connected to establishing peace. One of these issues was education. They agreed that Education for All is part of the key to a peaceful world. If all children received at least six to eight years of quality education, they would be able to read and write for a lifetime. And with literacy comes the possibility of a better world.

Leaders from Middle Eastern and African nations listen to the opening session of the United Nations Millennium Summit. These world leaders gathered together in hopes of creating a better world.

But in the year 2000, some 130 million children would never attend a school of any kind.[3] And another 145 million would drop out before they ever learned to read and write. That's 275 million children without an education.[4] How many is 275 million? Imagine if the entire population of the United States—every man, woman, and child—were not educated. That's how many children in the world did not get an education in the year 2000. Most of these 275 million children will never learn to read or write. And with this lifelong illiteracy comes poverty, poor health, homelessness, and hunger.

Bad News, Good News

World leaders at the UN Millennium Summit agreed that everyone on Earth should and could be educated. And they even set a target date of 2015. By then, they declared, "Children everywhere, boys and girls alike, will be able to complete a full course of primary schooling, and girls and boys will have equal access to all levels of education."[5]

Each country was supposed to make a plan to realize this goal of Education for All by 2015, then put the people and funds into place to put this plan into action.

The same thing had also happened ten years earlier. At another UN meeting in 1990 in the Southeast Asian country of Thailand, world leaders also called for Education for All. At that meeting they set the year 2000 as the target date. More than one hundred governments made plans, but when 2000 arrived, the goal of Education for All was still far from a reality.

Now, at the Millennium Summit, world leaders had moved the date forward to 2015. Would they do better this time? One education expert expressed his doubts when he wrote of "the unwillingness of governments the world over to fund public education properly."[6]

That's the bad news. But there is good news as well. Other forces are forming partnerships with governments around the world to help achieve Education for All. These forces include international agencies, such as the United Nations and the World Bank. They also include charities, labor unions, churches, and neighborhood social groups. This book is about these new forces and their struggles to make the goal of Education for All a reality.

Chapter 1

275 Million Short of Perfect

Nearly all the estimated 275 million children who are not getting a basic education live in the poor countries of Asia, Latin America, the Middle East, and Africa. These countries make up the developing world. They are called *developing* because they're striving to develop higher standards of living.

How wide is the gap between the world's rich and poor nations? The richest one-fifth of the world's people consume 86 percent of the world's wealth. Most of these people live in the industrialized nations, such as the United States. The poorest one-fifth consume just 1 percent. Most of these people live in the developing world.[1]

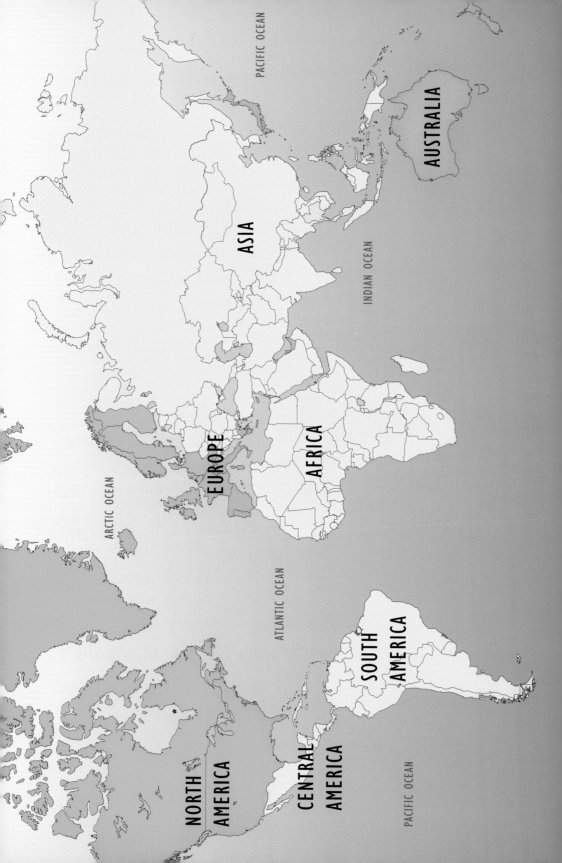

Map Opposite

The developing world is made up of poor countries in Asia, South and Central America, the Middle East, and Africa. Here, the many developing countries located around the world are highlighted in light orange.

Not Enough Money

How does this gap between rich and poor affect education? Governments fund public education. In the United States, for example, money to build and run public schools comes from federal, state, and local governments. The money is collected through taxes. A certain amount of tax money goes to each school.

Developing countries spend far less money on public education than industrialized nations spend. How much less?

- Industrialized nations spend an average of $4,636 to educate a student each year.

- Developing countries spend an average of $165 to educate a student each year.[2]

Why is so little money spent on education in the developing world? Birthrates are highest in the poorest countries. Rising population means rising demand for government services, such as clean water, electricity, and education. Governments in poor countries

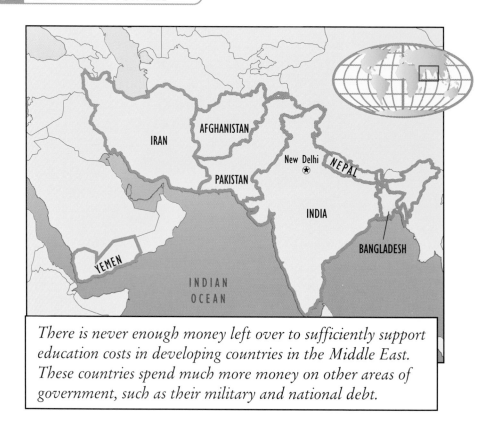

There is never enough money left over to sufficiently support education costs in developing countries in the Middle East. These countries spend much more money on other areas of government, such as their military and national debt.

already have more people than their country can support. They don't have the money to keep up with these rising demands.

Another reason is mounting debt. Rich nations have loaned billions of dollars to poor countries, loans that these countries can't possibly pay back. Some poor countries spend more trying to repay these loans than they spend on education.

One more reason is armed conflict. The governments of poor countries are less stable than the governments of rich nations. The less stable a government,

Because there is not enough funding for schools and other education costs, some students in India are taught outside without schoolhouses, desks, or even books.

the more conflicts that country will get into. Some poor countries spend more money on weapons and wars than they spend on education.

In 2000, for example, Pakistan's government spent six times as much on armies and weapons as it spent on primary education, while neighboring India spent nearly twice as much. Yet 11 million children in Pakistan and 30 million children in India were not in school.[3] A student interviewed in India's capital city of New Delhi asked, "If the government has money to explode nuclear bombs, why doesn't it have money to build schools?"[4] India and Pakistan were not at war, but they were longtime enemies. Each country was developing nuclear weapons to defend itself in case war should break out with its neighbor. Meanwhile, money sorely needed for new schools and teachers was not available.

Not Enough Classrooms or Teachers

Since developing countries are short of money for education, they are short of classrooms. People who build and manage schools try their best to make up for this shortage with ingenuity and resourcefulness. So it's not too surprising that classrooms in the developing world come in a variety of shapes and sizes.

There are many different types of classrooms that have been created in developing countries. These primary school students in Nigeria, eastern Africa, share desks in a schoolhouse with a dirt floor.

In a makeshift classroom in Zambia, southern Africa, young orphans are taught about important health issues such as AIDS.

For example, in a village in the South Asian country of Bangladesh, school may be a rented room in a family's home. The roof is tin, the walls are bamboo and mud, and the floor is packed earth. The children sit on bamboo mats holding slate boards on their knees. A metal trunk doubles as the teacher's desk and supply cabinet.

In a school in Mozambique, in southern Africa, there are only six classrooms for 924 students. The students attend school in three shifts, or separate groups, each day. These overused classrooms are worn-out and

Some classes are made up of students of all ages who are willing to learn under the most difficult circumstances.

run-down, like many classrooms in the developing world.

Teachers are in short supply as well. In Shyamolia School in Bangladesh, two teachers handle 370 students at a time. One teacher said, "There are so many students in each class that by the time I've called the roll and said hello, it's time to leave and go to the next class. What time do I have left to teach in?"[5]

Chapter 2

Partnerships for Change

Most governments in the developing world do not have enough money to fund public education by themselves. They need help, and help has been coming from a variety of groups.

Starting in the 1970s, groups dedicated to the UN goal of Education for All began forming. These groups include charities, foundations, unions, social clubs, businesses, and churches. Many are dedicated to a specific cause, such as saving rain forests, ending hunger in the world, and providing people with an education.

Many of these groups are partly funded by national governments. But since these groups are not part of any government, they are called nongovernment

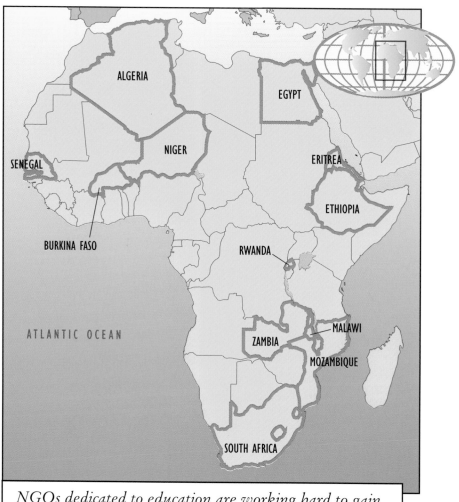

ALGERIA

EGYPT

NIGER

SENEGAL

ERITREA

ETHIOPIA

BURKINA FASO

RWANDA

ATLANTIC OCEAN

MALAWI

ZAMBIA

MOZAMBIQUE

SOUTH AFRICA

NGOs dedicated to education are working hard to gain funding for many countries throughout Africa. The countries that are discussed in this book are labeled here.

organizations (NGOs). By 1998 there were 40,000 NGOs worldwide, with hundreds dedicated to Education for All.[1] These groups work in partnership with governments and local communities to build and run schools in the developing world.

Schools That Fit the Community

Partnerships between NGOs and governments are responsible for thousands of new schools in the developing world. Many are built in rural areas that never saw a school before. For example, partnership schools serve 28,000 children in Burkina Faso, West Africa.[2]

Partnership schools are different from traditional, government-run schools. Most government schools are run by a one-size-fits-all plan: a single set of rules and regulations. But partnership schools are different. Each one is planned, built, and run by members of the local community to fit that community's unique needs.

Teachers from the Community

Teachers are in short supply in the developing world, especially in rural areas. Most people in the developing world live in rural communities, where people are poor. So partnership schools in rural communities can't afford to hire experienced teachers, who can make more money teaching in cities. Instead, partnership schools must hire members of the local community to teach.

These local teachers often are not experienced professionals. To make their job easier, students are in charge of their own learning. The learning materials are self-instructional (the instructions the student needs to do the work are contained in the materials). Students can do their work without a teacher to guide them. When students need help, they can get it from

Five NGOs Dedicated to Education for All

Education International (EI) is an organization of teachers' unions representing 24.5 million teachers and education workers worldwide. It is based in Brussels, Belgium. EI representatives meet with world leaders to persuade them to work for Education for All in the developing world.[3]

Oxfam (Oxford Committee for Famine Relief) is an international charity that supplies equipment and experts to help plan new schools in the developing world. It is based in Oxford, England. Oxfam insists that local community members build and run the schools themselves. With community control, Oxfam says, schools have a better chance of success.[4]

CIET (Centro de Investigación de Enfermedades Tropicales, or Tropical Disease Research Centre) is an interna-

other students. That's because several grade levels are taught in the same classroom, so older students can tutor younger students.

Success Follows Success

When a partnership school is successful, it becomes a model. Then more new schools like it are built in other communities to serve more and more students. In

tional group of research scientists based in New York. Teams of researchers survey communities in developing countries. They interview community members about how well their children are being educated. Other NGOs use CIET surveys to help plan schools that meet the needs of the local community.[5]

EDUCO plans and builds schools in the Central American country of El Salvador. EDUCO members work with support from the government of El Salvador. They use survey information from CIET and loans to El Salvador from the World Bank to help build new schools.[6]

Save the Children is an international relief organization based in Connecticut. This organization works in forty-five countries, including the United States. Its mission is to protect and care for children in emergency situations. Save the Children works with the UN and various governments to set up temporary schools for children in refugee camps.[7]

1991, EDUCO schools in El Salvador served 8,000 students. By 1999, they were serving 237,000.[8]

Model schools have been multiplying in developing countries all over the world, bringing education to remote rural communities that never had schools before. Some of the poorest and hardest-to-reach children are now students in partnership schools of various kinds.

Chapter 3

Children Left Behind Because of Who They Are

Partnership schools are making a difference, but the developing world still needs thousands more classrooms. But even if there were enough classrooms, millions of children would still be denied an education. These are the children who suffer discrimination because of who they are.

The largest group to suffer discrimination is girls. Worldwide, 42 million fewer girls attend primary school than boys. In one province of the South Asian country of Pakistan, for instance, 70 percent of boys attend school and only 45 percent of girls.[1] The problem is more serious in rural areas than in cities. In rural areas of the Middle Eastern country of

Egypt, for instance, only 12 girls attend school for every 100 boys.[2]

The United Nations calls discrimination against girls the largest single obstacle to achieving Education for All.[3] The roots of this discrimination lie in attitudes and traditions that are centuries old.

Sons Before Daughters

In the developing world, education is seldom free and often costly. Poor families must sacrifice to send a child to school. When it comes to choosing between sending a son or a daughter, the son will most likely be chosen.

Girls are discriminated against throughout many developing countries. In Thailand and other countries, there are a much larger number of boys who attend school than girls.

Why are boys chosen over girls? An educator in the Southeast Asian country of Thailand said, "If parents must choose, they would prefer to send their sons to school. They feel that girls don't need education as they will get married and raise families."[4]

Many parents in India feel the same way. When a girl marries, she moves in with the husband's family. Any money she earns goes to his family, not hers. So in India there is a well-known saying: "Educating a daughter is like watering another man's garden."

Stay-at-Home Attitude

In the Central Asian country of Afghanistan, some people still follow an ancient code of behavior known as *Pushtunwali*. According to this code, a woman may travel outside the home only if she is with a male relative. Women do not work outside the home, and girls do not attend school.

In Afghanistan, an eleven-year-old girl earns money with her mother by washing clothes for other people.

Girls in other parts of the developing world are also expected to stay at home. They help with housework and care for younger brothers and sisters, leaving them little or no time for school.

Boys Favored in the Classroom

Even girls who are sent to school have a hard time staying in school. In Pakistan, for example, girls are 40 percent more likely to drop out of school than boys.[5]

Why do so many girls drop out?

School is supposed to raise students' self-confidence, but many girls find the classroom a discouraging place. Most of the teachers in developing world schools are male. Surveys show that the majority of these teachers believe that boys are naturally better at math and science than girls. So these teachers give boys more attention and encouragement, which makes girls feel inferior and out-of-place.

Closing the Gender Gap

That's the bad news about girls and education.

But there is good news too. In many developing countries the gender gap is slowly closing. Gender gap is the difference between the number of boys and girls. Each year there are more girls in developing world schools than the year before.

Partnership schools are helping to bring more girls into the classroom by lowering costs. Community members build and run many partnership schools themselves. Sometimes they hire local teachers, who work for less. This means that it can cost less to educate a child in a partnership school than in a government-run school. So fewer parents have to choose between sending a son or a daughter. Now they can afford to send both.

Partnership schools in Burkina Faso, West Africa, help girls who have to look after younger brothers and sisters. They include free child-care centers, known as *Bisongos*, which help to bring more girls from their homes into the classroom.[6]

Boosting girls' self-confidence is another way of helping to close the gender gap. FAWE (Forum of African Women Educators) is an NGO set up by women in Africa who have risen to positions of authority in education.[7] The women of FAWE travel around Africa speaking to schoolgirls in rural areas about the advantages of getting an education. These women inspire as many girls as they can to enroll and stay in school and build better lives for themselves. They also raise money for scholarships to send girls from low-income families to school.

The women of FAWE point out how important it is to hire more female teachers. In rural areas, they say, school is the only place where girls can meet female authority figures other than family members. And surveys show that young girls feel more comfortable being taught by female teachers.

Partnership schools in the developing world have been hiring more female teachers. In the Middle Eastern country of Iran, more women have been trained to teach in rural areas. The results are encouraging. As of the year 2000, 96 percent of Iranian girls eligible for primary school were attending school.

How important is it for girls to get a good education? United Nations official Carol Bellamy says, "In study after study, girls' education emerges as the single best investment that any society can make. Educated girls become educated women—women who participate in the social, economic and political life of their nation."[8]

Ethnic Minorities

In the developing world, many languages may be spoken in one country. In many government schools in developing countries, classes are taught in one official language. In some countries, such as South Africa, that language is English.[9] In others, it is the language spoken by the majority of people.

What happens, then, to children of ethnic minorities? For these children, the official language is not the language they speak at home. In the Southeast Asian country of Vietnam, most people speak Kihn. Thirteen percent of the population speaks other, ethnic minority languages, yet Kihn is the only language used in schools.[10]

As a result, children of ethnic minorities have high dropout rates. Because classes are not taught in their

In the Latin American country of Bolivia, the educational materials that children use in schools are all in Spanish. Yet 60 percent of the people speak one of nine other native languages. These other native languages are ignored in the schools.

home language, the odds are low that these children will learn to read and write.

Some partnership and government schools deal with this discrimination by hiring teachers from the community. These teachers teach in the local language and use special learning materials printed in that language. In these schools, ethnic minorities no longer suffer discrimination because of who they are, and student attendance has increased.

Chapter 4

Children Left Behind Because of Where They Live

Another problem standing in the way of Education for All concerns geography. Millions more children in the developing world miss out on an education because of where they live.

Children living in rural areas are twice as likely not to attend school as those in cities. Niger, in northern Africa, is an example. In Niamey, Niger's capital city, more than 90 percent of children attend school. In rural areas, the figure drops to 20 percent.[1]

Distance from School

One reason for low school attendance in rural areas is distance. In the rural areas of most developing countries, the only way to travel is on foot through rough country. Half the rural families in the developing world live more than 6 miles (10 km) from a school.[2] In a town in the Philippines, for example, it is a four-hour walk over steep, rough trails to reach the school. Children of ethnic minorities are especially hard-hit by distance. They tend to live in the most remote, mountainous areas of developing countries.

Girls are also hard-hit, but for another reason. Traditionally, girls in the developing world lead sheltered lives. While boys are encouraged to get out and explore the world around them, girls are told to keep close to home. So a short distance for a boy is considered a long distance for a girl.

The farther the distance to school, the fewer the number of girls who attend. In Egypt, for instance, the average enrollment rate is 94 percent for boys and 74 percent for girls. This is for communities within 0.6 mile (1 km) of a school. When the distance to school is doubled to 1.2 miles (2 km), what happens? Boys' enrollment barely falls at all, but girls' enrollment drops by another 10 percent.[3]

Dangers Along the Way

Traveling even short distances in the developing world can be dangerous for girls and boys alike. During the rainy season, floods wash away paths, and shallow streams turn to rivers. This means that schools can close for weeks at a time.

Other dangers include tigers and poisonous snakes. In rural areas of Zambia, in southern Africa, rainy-season floods also close schools, and so do wild animals. Villagers living along a game reserve say they keep children at home for fear of wild animals attacking them on the way to school.

Communities in Motion

Movement makes it hard for children of nomads to get an education. Nomads move from place to place because their work is herding livestock, such as cattle or sheep. They move their herds according to the seasons, from upland pastures in the summer to lowland pastures in the winter.

Since they live in camps in remote areas and move with the seasons, nomad children are seldom near enough a school to get to it. And they must work several hours a day helping to tend the herds and to care for younger sisters and brothers.

Schools Come to Children

How do educators deal with these distance and movement problems? What strategies do they use to reach these hard-to-reach children?

In some developing countries, such as Iran, the children of nomads attend schools that move along with them. Each teacher is a member of the nomad community. First the teacher takes a training course sponsored by the UN. Then the teacher returns to the community with a school tent and teaching materials. This tent school is set up in the nomad camp and moves along with the camp wherever it goes.

Some children in remote areas don't have to go to school because school comes to them. The teacher brings "school" in a backpack. In the Cordillera Mountains in the Philippines, for example, teachers trek into remote mountainous areas. These mobile teachers bring schooling to children who would not have it otherwise.

In the Southeast Asian country of Cambodia there are villages that float. These villages are fishing communities of houseboats on freshwater lakes. Instead of sidewalks and roads, there are waterways between the bamboo homes.

One of these lakes is Tonle Sap, which means "Great Lake." On this lake is Kampong Prahok school. It is a houseboat moored among the floating homes. During the rainy season, the homes move to more sheltered waters. When the homes move, the school building moves with them. The students, who wear uniforms of white shirts and navy-blue skirts or trousers, paddle to school in canoes.

Kampong Prahok is one of several floating schools in Cambodia. The first ones were built in 1993 thanks to a partnership formed by the Cambodian government and the United Nations. Like the tent schools of

The people of this fishing village on the Mekong River in Cambodia live in floating bamboo homes, which are seen in the background.

Kampong Prahok school is a houseboat moored among the floating homes of Cambodia. Inside is a teacher's office with modern equipment and two classrooms that can hold up to eighty students.

Iran and the backpack-toting mobile teachers of the Philippines, the floating schools of Cambodia bring schooling to children in hard-to-reach places.

Distance Learning

Some students are scattered over too wide a distance to be reached by live, in-the-flesh teachers. So governments reach out to these students through distance learning. Instead of a live teacher, students learn through radio, audiocassettes, and the Internet.

Nepal broadcasts a series of radio programs for preschool children and their parents in remote mountain

In Australia, pockets of farming families are scattered over distances too vast to be reached by ordinary schools. Instead, children use a network of learning centers equipped with educational materials and computers from money supplied by the Australian government. There is no teacher on site, but students can contact teachers by the Internet for individual help.

The mountain villages in Nepal are very isolated from the more populated areas of the country. The students in these villages listen to radio programs that teach them and their parents.

villages. The radio show has a cast of characters that includes a talking bird and a pet elephant. These characters entertain children and supply parents with important information about health and nutrition.

Some developing countries, such as Bolivia, use a learning method known as IRI (interactive radio instruction). The IRI audio teacher does most of the actual teaching on radio or audiocassettes. The classroom teacher, who is in the schoolroom with the students, helps them follow the audio teacher's instructions and provides follow-up activities. While some students are listening to the radio or cassettes, the classroom teacher has time to work directly with other students.

Chapter 5

No Money, No Time

Public education in the developing world is seldom free. Parents pay for books, uniforms, paper, and pencils. Some government schools demand that parents pay as much as 70 percent of the cost of their children's education.

This cost is even higher for families who must pay extra, unofficial fees. These so-called extra fees are

Map Opposite

In Nicaragua and other Latin American countries, the cost of bribes that parents must pay educators prevents children from attending school. The Latin American countries discussed in this book are labeled here.

NICARAGUA

EL SALVADOR

CARIBBEAN SEA

COLOMBIA

PACIFIC
OCEAN

BOLIVIA

ATLANTIC
OCEAN

really bribes. Sometimes these bribes are paid with money. Sometimes they are paid with work—children doing housework for their teachers. Often, this happens because the teachers are underpaid. Nearly 70 percent of educators worldwide live at or below the poverty level.[1]

In a survey by CIET in the Central American country of Nicaragua, 86 percent of parents said they had to pay bribes to teachers.[2] Surveys in other developing countries showed similar results. Many of the parents surveyed said that these unofficial fees kept them from sending their children to school.

Reducing Fees

Partnership schools reduce fees as much as possible by reducing the schools' operating costs. Some government schools have followed this example. In 1994 the government of Malawi, in southern Africa, took a bold step. It made primary schooling free of charge for all children. The result was an immediate leap in enrollment from 1.9 million to 3.2 million. Three years later the government of the nearby country of Uganda did the same, and enrollments nearly doubled.[3]

These gains in enrollment brought on their own problems. Many new teachers would have to be hired, and many more new schools would have to be built. But these gains represented a step forward in education for the children of these developing countries.

Earning Over Learning

Many families in the developing world earn barely enough to survive. For these families, education is a luxury they cannot afford. The children in these families must spend their days earning money at work instead of learning in school.

"In developing countries, some 250 million children between the ages of five and fourteen must go to work outside the home," said Ambassador Nancy Rubin, head of the U.S. delegation to the UN Com-

Thousands of children in Afghanistan must work full-time outside the home to support themselves. This young person in the capital city of Kabul washes cars to earn a living.

mission on Human Rights.[4] That's one child out of every four. These are not children taking after-school jobs to earn extra money. These children work long hours every day to help support their families.

About half of these children must work full time.[5] They work as street vendors, factory laborers, domestic servants, car-wash boys, and streetcar conductors. Some 50 to 60 million are engaged in hazardous occupations, such as mining coal and picking through garbage dumps.[6] Most of this out-of-house work goes to boys. Girls tend to work in the home and in farm fields doing domestic chores or making things to sell.

Schools for Working Children

Many children work during normal school hours. A boy in Mumbai, India, said, "I work at the docks with many other children every morning. Some of us shell fish, others take them off the boats to shore. It is hard work. We have to be out before dawn when many people are still asleep."[7]

This boy attends a partnership school set up especially for children who work during the day. He attends one of the Door Step schools in the slums of Mumbai. Door Step schools were started in 1989 by a combination of NGOs and government agencies from India, Japan, Britain, and Canada.

Each school is carefully planned. First, Door Step officials surveyed the community. Survey results showed that both boys and girls worked long hours at all different times of the day. So Door Step schools offer classes at night as well as during the day. Today there are thirty of these schools reaching 1,700 working children in Mumbai. The boy from the docks said, "Now I attend classes in the afternoon where we learn how to read, write, and count. I also visit a small library where we can read storybooks. I study quite hard and want to be a navy officer. I see many officers in smart white uniforms. They work on big ships out in the distance."[8]

Schooling at Door Step is outside of the official government school system. Children do not receive credit leading to a diploma as they do in official government schools. The boy at the docks wants to move on to a government school someday, so that he can graduate and join the navy. Door Step teachers help give children the basic skills they need to move on to regular schooling and a career.

Besides conventional classrooms, Door Step operates a School-on-Wheels. This bus goes out to hard-to-reach students, such as children of families who live and work at construction sites. The bus carries books and learning materials. The driver is the teacher, who holds classes inside the bus.

Making the Curriculum Relevant

Most people in the developing world live in small villages and earn their living by farming and raising livestock. But in most government-run schools, students don't learn about agriculture or raising animals. They don't learn about the life in their village or gain skills that will help them make a living as adults. A teacher from India said, "The curriculum is drastically at variance with the life these children lead. For these children, school does not open up a new world of learning and knowledge."[9]

The curriculum is not relevant to their lives. As a result, some children choose work over school. A ten-year-old shoeshine boy from Senegal, in western Africa, said, "I don't need to go to school. What can I learn there? I know children who went to school. Their family paid for the fees and the uniforms and now they are educated. But you see them sitting around. Now they are useless to their families. They don't know anything about farming or trading or making money. If anyone tries to put me in school I will run away."[10]

Partnership schools are making the curriculum more relevant to children's lives. In Colombia, South America, thousands of partnership schools known as Escuela Nueva operate in rural areas. One reason these schools are successful is their curriculum. They offer a relevant curriculum that teaches students what they want and need to know.

One Escuela Nueva student said, "What we want is to feel proud of being country people and to learn how to use the land in a more productive way."[11] Escuela Nueva teachers visit children's homes and collect proverbs, myths, legends, and stories about the history of the community. They collect family recipes and

These students at an Escuela Nueva in Colombia work on a community-related lesson together.

songs and samples of homemade arts and crafts. They collect information about the work people do and the games they play. Then they use this information as a basis for teaching in school.

Partnership schools in other developing countries have done the same. The result is a curriculum that teaches basic skills that relate to the community where the students live. Enrollment in partnership schools in developing world countries has increased as a result.

Chapter 6

Home, Health, Hunger

The world leaders at the UN Millennium Summit agreed that education must take place in a safe, secure environment free from violence. But in much of the developing world, widespread violence is part of daily life. According to UN estimates, 540 million children—one in every four, or 25 percent of the world's youth—live in dangerous and unstable conditions. Between 1990 and 2000, 2 million children were killed in armed conflicts, while 6 million more were injured or disabled. Another estimated 300,000 children were directly involved in fighting as child soldiers in the year 2000.[1]

In the Midst of Conflict

Armed conflict leads to a breakdown of society. And when society breaks down, education breaks down. Schools are destroyed and teachers are killed. In Mozambique, in southern Africa, more than two-thirds of the school buildings were destroyed in civil wars. During a recent civil war in Rwanda, in central Africa, an estimated 60 percent of the nation's teachers were murdered.[2]

In some developing countries, teachers and students live for years in a state of fear. In Colombia, South America, for example, a civil war has been raging since 1980. Many small army units are fighting each other. These armies use schools as bases of operation. When

In Somalia, eastern Africa, classes are held in buildings destroyed by civil war.

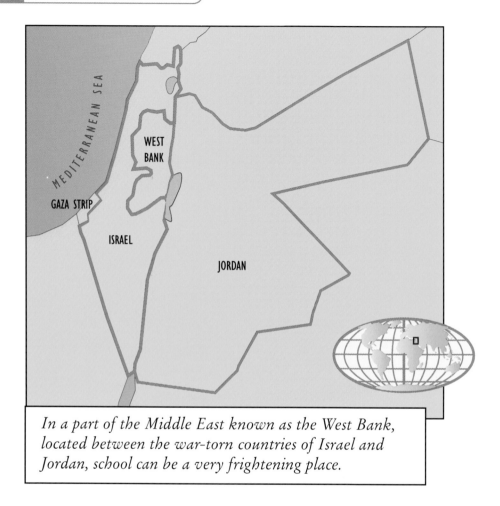

In a part of the Middle East known as the West Bank, located between the war-torn countries of Israel and Jordan, school can be a very frightening place.

one army moves out of the area, another one moves in. Between 1986 and 2001 in Colombia, more than 400 teachers were killed.[3]

Palestinian students and teachers in the Al-Sharka school for girls also live in a state of fear. The school is located in a part of the Middle East known as the West Bank, between Jordan and Israel. For decades the Palestinians and Israelis have fought for possession of the West Bank. On some days students can see the fighting from their desks. One day, Israeli tear gas flooded the school, sending dozens of students to the hospital. For these children, and for millions of others in the developing world, school can be a fearful place.

Like hospitals, churches, and government buildings, schools are symbols of order and stability. Even in the midst of war, people try hard to keep schools open and operating. One such school is in Fatsi, a village in Ethiopia, northern Africa. Fatsi is near the border with Eritrea, Ethiopia's enemy in a war that began in 1998. Since then, the Fatsi primary school has been forced to move three different times to escape the violence. One of the school's locations was a cave. Stu-

In Fatsi, Ethiopia, students attend classes held in a cave up in the mountains to protect themselves from the violent war that surrounds their village.

dents had to trek up a steep footpath between cliffs to a rocky plateau. Then they stepped inside the cave where they were safe, for the time being, from the shooting outside.

Forced to Flee

Every day, people in developing countries flee their homes because of war. Some make their way to another country as refugees. People become refugees only as a last resort. They leave their homeland in order to survive.

Imagine fleeing your home, your town, your nation, in fear for your life. Imagine seeking shelter in a country of strangers where hardly anyone speaks your language. You have little or no money and few, if any, possessions. Imagine having to start life over from scratch as a stranger in a strange land. This is the challenge that refugee families, including children, must face.

Schools for Refugees

How do refugees begin to make a new life?

After food, clothing, and shelter, refugees seek schooling. New schools are a sign that life is returning to normal. Learning gives people hope. And refugees have a lot to learn quickly. They must learn the language and customs of the nation they have fled to. They must also continue to learn their own language and customs for when they return to their homeland.

Partnership organizations work with the UN to set up special schools in refugee camps. For example, a school can be as simple as stones and logs for school desks arranged in rows beneath a tree.

A number of schools have been set up for Afghan refugees in Pakistan. For Afghan girls, there is one good thing about their refugee status. At home, the code of *Pushtunwali* kept them out of school. In Pakistan, they gain the right to schooling. In these schools for Afghan refugees, girls make up more than 20 percent of the students.[4]

Afghan refugee girls attend all-girl classes taught by Afghan women who are also refugees. These women are

In January 2002, Afghan refugee girls attend school in Pakistan. Many Afghan girls who have arrived at Pakistan refugee camps are attending class for the first time in their lives.

World Refugee Profile

Number of refugees: The UN reported a total of 21 million refugees in the year 2000, or one out of every 284 persons worldwide.[5] Most live in refugee camps under perilous conditions. Some will return to their homeland one day. Many will not.

Largest producer of refugees: Afghanistan has led the world in producing refugees since the early 1980s, when a long war with neighboring Russia began. Between 1980 and 2000, an estimated 3.7 million Afghans were forced to flee their homeland.[6] After the September 11, 2001, terrorist attacks on the United States, American forces bombed terrorist bases in Afghanistan. More Afghans tried to flee their country to escape the bombing. But many of them were held back when neighboring countries sealed off their borders with Afghanistan.

trained by UN workers. Their learning materials include Edukits, also known as schools-in-a-box. Edukits include pens, a chalkboard, chalk, crayons, erasers, exercise booklets, paper, glue, pencils, and a pencil sharpener. Edukits are distributed by the UN and paid for by donations from NGOs and governments.

Countries taking in refugees: Most refugees flee to neighboring countries. In 2000, more refugees fled to Pakistan than anywhere else. Among them were 800,000 Afghans.[7] Many Afghan refugees also fled to neighboring Iran. As of 2001, an estimated 1.5 million Afghan refugees lived in Iran and an estimated 2 million Afghan refugees lived in Pakistan.[8]

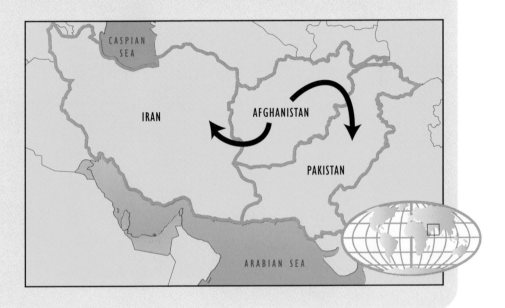

Schools for Displaced Children

IDPs, internally displaced persons, are not refugees. They leave their homes but not their homeland. IDPs migrate to another part of their country. Some migrate to escape wars or natural disasters. Others leave to make a better life for themselves. Every day more and more rural people in developing countries migrate from the country to the city. They migrate in hope that cities will offer them better jobs and better schooling.

China is a good example. Rural families who migrate to cities in China are known as the floating population, or floaters. Some will return to the countryside. Others will remain in cities. The Chinese government estimates the number of floaters at 100 million.[9] Some live crowded together with relatives or

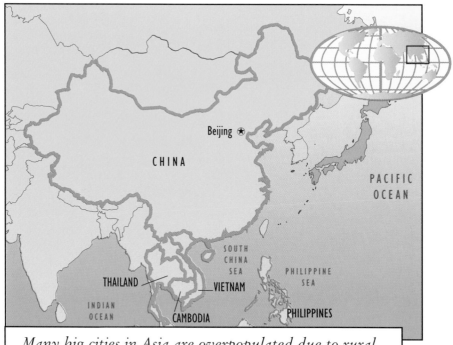

Many big cities in Asia are overpopulated due to rural families migrating to find better jobs and better schools. Due to overcrowding, China's capital city, Beijing, has forbidden migrating children to attend formal schools.

friends. Others live in shacks built from whatever materials they can find.

Millions of floaters have migrated to the capital city of Beijing, making the city overcrowded. City officials want to discourage more floaters from coming. So floater children are forbidden to attend the official, government-run schools in Beijing.

But unofficial schools have been opened for children of the floating population. Beijing has several hundred floater schools. Schools for floater, or migrant, children have sprung up in other developing countries as well. NGOs run these schools, with help from the United Nations and other donors.

Health Hazards

Children who are ill have a hard time learning. Health hazards such as malaria, iodine deficiency, and parasitic worms are rare in the industrialized world. But in the developing world, health hazards like these are common and sometimes deadly.

The most serious and deadly health hazard in the developing world is the AIDS epidemic. Africa has suffered worst of all. More than 8 million children aged fourteen or younger have lost one or both parents to AIDS in Africa.[10] The effect of AIDS on education has been devastating. In Zambia, in southern Africa, 1,300 teachers died from AIDS in 1998 alone.

Many areas in the developing world don't have water that's safe to drink or food that's safe to eat. This can

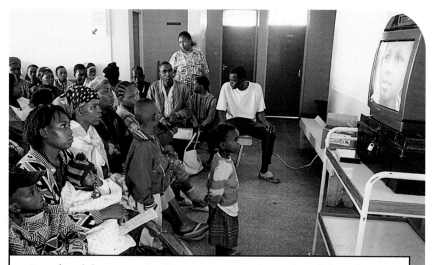

At a health center in Kenya, east Africa, local families watch an AIDS awareness video.

Orphaned children attend class at the Fountain of Hope center in Zambia, southern Africa. Fountain of Hope is a relief agency that cares for orphans from the town of Lusaka, which has been destroyed by the AIDS epidemic.

lead to deadly consequences. The resulting health problems, such as diarrhea, usually amount to no more than mild discomforts in the industrialized world. But in the developing world, these health problems can be fatal.

Sometimes schools themselves add to the problem. Many schools in the developing world expose children to unhealthy conditions. In the Middle Eastern country of Yemen, for instance, half the schools do not have access to safe water. In Pakistan, 70 percent of the schools have no toilets.[11]

Health-Promoting Schools

NGOs, international organizations, and governments of developing countries are cooperating to create health-promoting schools. A health-promoting school actively promotes good physical and mental health for all students. The following list of characteristics is based on goals set by the World Health Organization and the United Nations.

Characteristics of a Health-Promoting School
- Teaches children good health and nutrition habits
- Has good sanitation facilities, including separate bathrooms for boys and girls, and access to safe water
- Is a place where diseases can be detected and treated
- Includes free health insurance and medical checkups for all children

- Is supportive of all, including children with special needs and children with the AIDS virus
- Is a place of safety, where teachers are protectors of children
- Teaches children how to make informed, healthy choices and to successfully negotiate and resolve conflicts
- Promotes each child's sense of well-being, self-confidence, and dignity

Dealing With Hunger

Children who are hungry have a hard time learning. Many hungry children can't attend school at all. They must spend all their time and energy trying to help their families survive. And hungry children who do attend school are often too weak and tired to learn.

NGOs work with the UN's World Food Program (WFP) to help feed schoolchildren. The WFP sends food surpluses from industrialized countries, such as the United States, to schools in the developing world. In Burkina Faso, for example, a food program sponsored by WFP was introduced. As a result, more children enrolled in school, and the dropout rate fell sharply. In Pakistan, enrollment tripled when food programs were introduced in two provinces in 1994. A WFP official says, "A snack or a hot meal at school not only gives children a break from their search for food, it also ensures that they are alert and concentrated in class."[12]

Chapter 7

Education in the United States

We have seen that problems with education are severe and widespread in developing countries. This is not the case in the industrialized world. Virtually every child receives an education. But it is not always a quality education that produces graduates who can read and write. The industrialized world has its own set of education problems to overcome.

Graduates Who Can't Read

The industrialized world includes the fourteen nations in the European Union as well as Australia, Canada, and the United States. In these nations, primary-school enrollment is nearly 100 percent.

Map Opposite

The industrialized world, shown here in dark orange, includes the richer nations of Australia, Canada, the United States, Japan, and parts of Europe. Although school enrollment is high in these countries, many students leave school unable to read and write.

But statistics show that many children leave school unable to read and write. In the United States, Great Britain, and Ireland, one of every five adults has serious problems with reading and writing. Many people in industrialized nations leave school without the skills necessary for finding and keeping a well-paying job.

Inner-City Problems

As we've seen, the most serious education problems in the developing world are concentrated in rural areas. Most people of the developing world still live in villages, where they grow and hunt their own food. But in the industrialized countries, a much smaller percentage of people make their living by raising crops and livestock.

The great majority of people live and work in towns, suburbs, and big cities. And that is where the most serious education problems in the United States are found, in the poorest sections of big cities such as New York, Chicago, and Los Angeles. A presidential report on nationwide reading test scores in 2001 states: "Today, nearly 70 percent of inner-city fourth graders are unable to read at a basic level on national reading tests."[1] The list on page sixty-two is based on a survey of tested students.

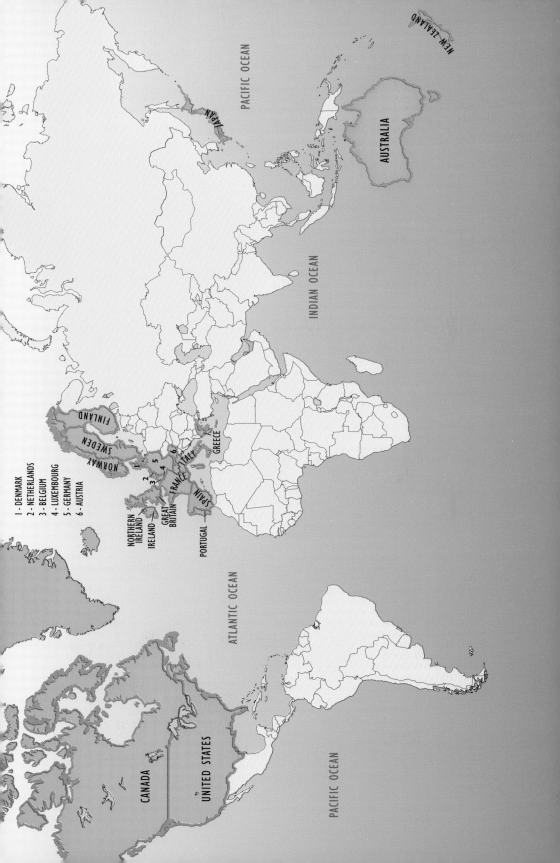

NEW ZEALAND

PACIFIC OCEAN

AUSTRALIA

JAPAN

INDIAN OCEAN

FINLAND

SWEDEN

NORWAY

GREECE

ITALY

FRANCE

SPAIN

1 - DENMARK
2 - NETHERLANDS
3 - BELGIUM
4 - LUXEMBOURG
5 - GERMANY
6 - AUSTRIA

NORTHERN
IRELAND

IRELAND

GREAT
BRITAIN

PORTUGAL

ATLANTIC OCEAN

CANADA

UNITED STATES

PACIFIC OCEAN

Characteristics of Low-Scoring Students
- Most live in poor urban neighborhoods.
- Most have changed schools within the last two years.
- 34 percent watch more than six hours of television every day.
- 57 percent said they have friends who make fun of people who try hard in school.[2]

U.S. Secretary of Education Rod Paige commented on these test results. He said they showed that children in low-income families, who most need quality education, are getting less of it, not more.

One of the reasons is money. Most of the funds to operate U.S. public schools come from taxes paid by

Many children in big cities cannot concentrate in school because their families are poor and hungry. Here, a church in Chicago offers disadvantaged children free meals at a place called the Kids Café.

local property owners. In the inner-city communities where low-income families live, property values are low. So these communities receive less money for education, on average, than wealthier suburban communities, where property values are higher. For instance, in 1994, the wealthiest 5 percent of Vermont's school districts spent $6,000 per student, while the poorest 5 percent spent less than half that.[3] This leaves low-income students with inferior facilities and educational materials and with fewer experienced teachers.

Positive Signs: Government Action

In January 2002, President George W. Bush signed into law the Elementary and Secondary Education Act. This new bill promises to see that the students who most need quality education start getting it.

Features of the Elementary and Secondary Education Act
- Provides more government money for public schools with large numbers of needy children
- Sets aside $900 million for needy schools to hire teachers to work with students who need extra help in reading[4]
- Sets aside additional money for teacher training
- Orders the states to see that public schools test their students regularly in reading and math to measure student performance

Schools whose students test poorly are labeled as failing schools. Failing schools have five years to improve students' test scores. In the meantime, these schools get more money to hire more teachers and buy new materials, such as textbooks and computers.

If a failing school does not improve, parents may transfer their children to another public school. If after five years a failing school still hasn't improved students' test scores, its teachers and principals may lose their jobs and be replaced. Or the school may be converted into a charter school.

Charter Schools

Charter schools are a different kind of public school. Like traditional public schools, they do not charge tuition. They receive their money from state and federal governments.

But charter schools do not have to follow all the rules and regulations that traditional public schools must follow.

Some charter schools are run by nonprofit, nongovernment organizations. Others are run for profit. The groups who run charter schools are free to choose their own curriculum and teachers. Each school is run a different way, according to the particular needs of the community it serves.

Some charter schools serve low-income, inner-city communities. The students in these communities have not done well in traditional public schools. Some have physical and mental disabilities. Some are homeless.

Some charter schools serve recent immigrants who speak little or no English. The Passages Charter School is one of these. Students at Passages come from families whose home languages include Arabic, Spanish, and Urdu, which is spoken by Muslims in India and Pakistan. Classes are taught in English, but teachers offer special help for students to whom English is a second language. The school features the refugee and immigrant experience in its social science and literature classes. Passages also offers counseling for all the members of students' families to help them adjust to life in a new country.

Some charter schools offer a specialized curriculum that attracts students from all over a city. The Charter School of the Chicago Children's Choir (CSCC) offers a curriculum for students with a special interest in music. Students learn to sing in as many as seventeen different languages. Besides teaching students to sing and play music, the school uses music to help teach other subjects. In social studies, for instance, students learn about the music of different cultures. The school's principal says, "We are really trying to thread music into every aspect of the day."[5]

Charter School Problems

The first charter school was created in 1992. By the year 2000 more than 2,000 charter schools were operating in thirty-four states, serving more than a half-million students.[6]

They promise students new and better ways of learning. Because charter schools are free of the rules and regulations that typical public schools must follow, they can practice different and innovative ways of learning. They can put new ideas about learning into action.

But this promise has not always worked out in practice. Arizona has more than 400 charter schools, more than any other state.[7] A look at Arizona's charter schools reveals problems that show up in charter schools in other states.

A key problem is a lack of new ideas. A former charter-school principal, Bill Scheel, says that only a handful of Arizona's 400 charter schools offer "instruction that is significantly different, either in content or in format, from the typical public school."[8]

Another problem is accountability. In Arizona, as in other states, information on charter-school performance is hard to come by. No one publishes lists of charter-school test scores, so charter-school performance cannot be compared with performance in other public schools.

In one state where test scores were compared, charter schools did not do well. A Texas report in 2000 found that the state's 200 charter schools had poor academic performance when compared with typical Texas public schools.[9]

Charter schools hold great promise for improving education in the United States. They have yet to live up to that promise.

Chapter 8

Moving Toward a Better World

Thanks to partnerships among world governments, nongovernment organizations, and international organizations such as the United Nations, there are signs of progress in worldwide education. More of the developing world's children are being educated each year. But progress is not fast enough to reach the UN goal of Education for All by 2015.

No Easy Fixes

This book began with the UN Millennium Summit and its goal that "children everywhere, boys and girls alike, will be able to complete a full course of primary

The United Nations Educational, Scientific, and Cultural Organization (UNESCO) sponsors schools for refugees of many countries.

schooling, and that girls and boys will have equal access to all levels of education."[1]

Experts agree that there are no easy fixes to reach this goal. The problems are too varied, too severe, and too deep-rooted to be overcome by any single strategy. And that includes money. Ever since the early 1970s, developing countries have been receiving a steady flow of aid from industrialized nations. Each year they receive billions of dollars in aid for education.

Most of this aid comes in the form of loans from governments and international banks. In a perfect world these loans would all be used to build new schools and to train and hire new teachers. But some of this money is wasted. Some of this waste comes from mismanagement: poor decisions by both borrowers and lenders on how to use the money. Some of this waste occurs when money is diverted from building schools to fighting wars.

In the meantime, loans from industrialized nations are not repaid. And for every day that loans remain unpaid, interest, or the cost of borrowing money, piles up. This drives the debt higher. Some developing countries owe so much money in loans that they will never be able to repay them.

Two Worlds, One Goal

Many problems remain to be solved before the goal of Education for All can be achieved. These problems are far more serious in the developing world than in the industrialized world. But dedicated people in both worlds have discovered similar strategies for attacking these problems. They examine each individual community and ask themselves: What kinds of schools can best serve these particular students and parents? How can public funds be more effectively spent to secure quality education for all children?

Then schools and school systems are designed to fit each community's unique needs. In the developing world, partnership schools are bringing education to communities and children who have never had it before. In the United States, the charter-schools movement and the Elementary and Secondary Education Act hold the promise of giving communities the quality education they've been missing.

How You Can Help

Each year young people in the industrialized world play a part in helping to achieve Education for All by volunteering their time and energy. Some help students in local schools. Others help students in schools in the developing world.

By Tutoring

You can help by volunteering time to tutor younger students. Some schools have in-school tutoring programs. Other schools have tutoring programs to help students in neighboring schools and children in daycare centers. Some suburban schools send students to inner-city schools to tutor low-income students. If your school doesn't have a tutoring program, you might speak to a teacher or your principal about getting one started. Students for Other Students, a nonprofit organization, offers help to students who want to establish tutoring programs. Their Web site is www.utoledo.edu/colleges/education/sos/main.html.

By Raising Money

You can help by raising money to build and improve schools in the developing world. Some students raise money through events such as car washes and bake sales, then donate the proceeds to organizations such as Save the Children and UNICEF.

Students in Ohio and California raised funds for a U.S. Department of Energy program that brings electric power to schools in Africa. Their funds helped purchase solar panels to generate electricity for schools in rural Uganda. The program, known as Village Power 2000, is described on the Web site at www.VillagePower2000.org.

By Volunteering

Volunteers of all ages help by traveling to a developing country to lend a hand in building a school. Several nonprofit programs run by churches and charitable organizations help build schools in rural areas of Mexico and Central America, where preteens and teenagers dig foundations, mix cement, lay bricks, and carry water. Some volunteers spend time teaching the local children.

One of these volunteer organizations is Seeds of Learning. Each year this organization sends youth groups to Central America to build rural schools. Their program is described on their Web site at www.seedsoflearning.org.

For Further Information

A great deal of information on Education for All is available on the World Wide Web. You can use a search engine, such as Google, Northern Light, or Yahoo, to call up lists of Web sites. Try some of these key words:

Education for All
nongovernment organizations
developing countries
charter schools
distance education

The following Web sites are especially good spots for picking up a broad range of information on different aspects of Education for All.

Center for Education Reform
www.edreform.com/
This NGO is dedicated to improving U.S. schools. The Web site includes information on U.S. charter schools nationwide.

Charter Schools Profiles
www.cps.k12.il.us/Schools/Opportunities/Charter/School_Profiles/school_profiles.html

This section of the Chicago Public Schools Web site has detailed information on sixteen inner-city charter schools. Each one has its own specialized curriculum and education objectives.

Global Movement for Children
www.gmfc.org/en/index_html
This worldwide organization of NGOs is dedicated to promoting the rights of the child. The Web site has sections on protecting children from war, disease, and hunger, and on educating every child.

United Nations Conference on Trade and Development
www.unctad.org/en/subsites/ldcs/country/country.htm
This section of this UN Web site gives statistical profiles of developing countries.

United Nations Cyberschoolbus
www.un.org/pubs/cyberschoolbus/
This UN Web site gives young people a look at how the United Nations works. It includes statistics on all the member nations.

The U.S. Department of Education
www.ed.gov/
This government Web site contains the latest news and information about education in the United States.

World Bank World Links for Development program
www.worldbank.org/html/schools/wlinks.htm
The World Bank is an international banking institution that lends money to developing countries. This section of their Web site describes a project that links students and teachers in secondary schools in developing countries with schools in industrialized countries for collaborative learning through the Internet.

End Notes

Introduction

1. Oxfam. Education Now. www.caa.org.au/oxfam/advocacy/education/report/chapter4-2.html, accessed January 12, 2001.
2. United Nations. United Nations Millennium Declaration. www.un.org/millennium/htm, September 18, 2000, p. 1.
3. UNICEF. State of the World's Children 2000 Education. www.unicef.org/sowc00/, p. 46.
4. Chris Brazier. Making It Happen. New Internationalist. www.oneworld.org/ni/issue315/keynote.htm, August 1999.
5. United Nations, United Nations Millennium Declaration, p. 5.
6. Chris Brazier. The Great Education Scandal. New Internationalist. www.oneworld.org/ni/issue315/keynote.htm, August 1999.

Chapter 1

1. Bread for the World. Hunger Basics: International Facts on Hunger and Poverty. www.bread.org/hungerbasics/international.html, accessed September 12, 2001.
2. Larry Elliott. Lesson the World Must Learn. Guardian Unlimited. www.guardian.co.uk/Archive/Article/0,4273,3841807,00.html, March 22, 1999.
3. Oxfam. Education Now. www.caa.org.au/oxfam/advocacy/education/report/chapter4-2.html, accessed January 12, 2001.
4. Chris Brazier. Making It Happen. New Internationalist. www.oneworld.org/ni/issue315/keynote.htm, August 1999.

5. Sameera Huque. Ideal & Reality. New Internationalist. www.oneworld.org/ni/issue315/ideal.htm, August 1999.

Chapter 2

1. Lester R. Brown and others. *State of the World 2001*. (Worldwatch Institute. New York: W.W. Norton & Company, 2001), p. 196.
2. UNICEF. Education Initiatives: Education Is a Right. www.unicef.org/programme/education/advcamp.htm, accessed August 4, 2001.
3. Education International. www.ei-ie.org, accessed August 2001.
4. Oxfam International. www.oxfaminternational.org, accessed August 2001.
5. CIET International. www.ciet.org, accessed August 2001.
6. United Nations Educational, Scientific, and Cultural Organization. Education and Poverty Eradication—El Salvador. www.unesco.org/education/poverty/el_salvador.shtml, accessed August 2001.
7. Save the Children. www.savethechildren.org, accessed August 2001.
8. The World Bank Group. El Salvador. www.wb1n0018.world-bank.org/external/lac/lac/nsf/694dc25670b0e31985267d6006a9c9e/8ea634511ffdc6578525695f004884dl?OpenDocument, accessed September 24, 2001.

Chapter 3

1. Charlotte Carlsson. A Quiet Escape. New Internationalist. www.oneworld.org/ni/issue315/quiet.htm, August 1999.
2. Victoria Brittain, Larry Elliott, and John Carvel. Learning Lies Out of Reach for 125m of the World's Poorest Children. Guardian Unlimited. www.guardian.co.uk/Archive/Article/0,4273,3956796,00.html, January 31, 2000.
3. UNICEF. The State of the World's Children 1999 Education. www.unicef.org/sowc99, p. 52.
4. Teena Gill. Thailand Fails Its Children. www.atimes.com/asia-crisis/AH17Db01.html, August 17, 1999.
5. Carlsson, A Quiet Escape.

6. UNICEF. Education Initiatives: Education Is a Right. www.unicef.org/programme/education/advcamp.htm, accessed August 4, 2001.
7. Forum for African Women Educationalists. www.fawe.org, accessed August 2001.
8. UNICEF. State of the World's Children 2000. www.unicef.org/sowc00/, p. 47.
9. Neville Alexander. Where English Can Serve But Not Empower. Guardian Unlimited. www.guardian.co.uk/Archive/article/0,4273,4115277,00.html, January 11, 2001.
10. Oxfam. Education Now. www.caa.org.au/oxfam/advocacy/education/report/chapter 2-3.html, accessed August 23, 2001.

Chapter 4

1. Oxfam. Education Now. www.caa.org.au/oxfam/advocacy/education/report/chapter 3-3.html, accessed August 23, 2001.
2. Victoria Brittain, Larry Elliott, and John Carvel. Learning Lies Out of Reach for 125m of the World's Poorest Children. Guardian Unlimited. www.guardian.co.uk/Archive/Article/0,4273,3956796,00.html, January 31, 2000.
3. Oxfam. Education Now. www.caa.org.au/oxfam/advocacy/education/report/chapter 4.html, accessed August 23, 2001.

Chapter 5

1. Education International. Global Campaign for Education. www.campaignforeducation.org/what_is/what_is.html, accessed August 2001.
2. Charlotte Carlsson. Invisible Burdens. Guardian Unlimited. www.guardian.co.uk/Archive/Article/0,4273,4026581,00.html, June 8, 2000.
3. Chris Brazier. Making It Happen. New Internationalist. www.oneworld.org/ni/issue315/keynote.htm, August 1999.
4. Department of State Washington File. Nancy Rubin April 11 Remarks to the U.N. Commission on Human Rights. www.usis-australia.gov/hyper/2000/0412/epf304.htm, April 11, 2000.
5. Education International, Global Campaign for Education.
6. UNICEF. State of the World's Children 2000. www.unicef.org/sowc00/, p. 24.

7. Door Step School—A Project for Working Slum Children. www.indiaworld.co.in/home/sahayata/doorstep.html, accessed September 10, 2001.

8. Door Step School—A Project for Working Slum Children.

9. Stephen Bates. Educating Gita. Guardian Unlimited. www. guardian.co.uk/Archive/Article/0,4273, 3973464,00.html, March 14, 2000.

10. Chris Brazier. Gender Canyon. New Internationalist. www.one world.org/ni/issue315/gender.htm, August 1999.

11. Asbel Lopez. Colombia Exports Its 'New School' Blueprint. UNESCO Courier. www.unesco.org/courier/1999_06/uk/ apprend/txt1.htm, June 1999.

Chapter 6

1. UNICEF. Effects of Military Conflict on Children. http://clubs.asua.arizona.edu/~amun/conference/2002/ committees/unicef/default.htm, accessed January 12, 2002.

2. Oxfam. Education Now. www.caa.org.au/oxfam/advocacy/ education/report/chapter 4-1.html, accessed January 12, 2001.

3. Harry Kelber. Death Lists in Colombia. The Labor Educator. www.laboreducator.org/dthcol.htm, June 25, 2001.

4. UNESCO. Refugee Education: More Afghan Girls In School. www.unesco.org/education/educprog/emergency/casestudy/ pakistan.htm, accessed January 5, 2002.

5. Europa World. 21 Million People Worldwide 'Of Concern' To UN Refugee Agency in Year 2000. www.europaworld.org/ Issue35/21millionpeopleworldwide18501.htm, May 18, 2001.

6. Human Rights Watch. Safe Refuge for Afghan Refugees. www. hrw.org/campaigns/afghanistan/refugees-facts.htm, accessed January 13, 2002.

7. Europa World. 21 Million People Worldwide 'Of Concern' To UN Refugee Agency in Year 2000.

8. Human Rights Watch. Safe Refuge for Afghan Refugees.

9. James Irwin. China's Migrant Children Fall Through the Cracks. UNESCO Courier. www.unesco.org/courier/2000_09/ uk/apprend.htm, September, 2000.

10. UNICEF. The State of the World's Children 1999 Education. www.unicef.org/sowc99, p. 55.

11. Oxfam. Education Now. www.caa.org.au/oxfam/advocacy/education/report/chapter 2-3.html, accessed January 12, 2001.
12. UNESCO. Food for Thought. www.unesco.org/education/educnews/99_10_01/schoolfeeding.htm, November 1, 1999.

Chapter 7

1. George W. Bush. No Child Left Behind. Executive Summary. www.ed.gov/inits/nclb/part2.html, accessed August 21, 2001.
2. Marguerite Roza. It's the Teachers, Stupid. Christian Science Monitor. www.csmonitor.com/durable/2001/04/19/text/p11s2.html, April 20, 2001.
3. School Reform News. Court Finds Vermont School Property Taxes Unconstitutional. www.heartland.org/education/mar97/court.htm, March 1997.
4. Diana Jean Schemo. "Education Bill Urges New Emphasis on Phonics as Method for Teaching Reading." (*New York Times*, January 9, 2002), p. A16.
5. Maria Kantzavelos. "1 Charter School Too Many in City." *Chicago Tribune*. www.chicagotribune.com/news/local/chi-0108080252aug28.story?coll=chi%2Dnews%2Dhed, August 8, 2001.
6. *New York Times*. "Blank Slate: The Story of a Charter School's First Year." www.nytimes.com/learning/general/specials/bronx prep/graphs.html, accessed November 2, 2001.
7. Bill Scheel. "Charter Schools' Bold Steps Falter in Reality's Light." (*Arizona Republic*, January 1, 2002), p. B7.
8. Scheel, p. B7.
9. Pat Kossan. "Charter Schools Face More Scrutiny." *Arizona Republic*. www.azcentral.com/news/education/1223charter nation23.html, December 23, 2001.

Chapter 8

1. United Nations. United Nations Millennium Declaration. www.un.org/millennium/htm, September 18, 2000, p. 5.

Index

Page numbers in *italics* refer to illustrations.